Timeless Thoughts of a Believer

Written by Rayaan

بِسْمِ اللهِ الرَّحْمَٰنِ الرَّحِيمِ
Bismillahir Rahmanir Raheem

timeless thoughts

i found my faith again,
when i realised,
Allah doesn't forsake,
the believer.

timeless thoughts of a believer

why am i here?
what is my purpose?
and where am i going?

timeless thoughts

i got so caught up,
in this dunya,
that i forgot Allah,
it's one of my deepest regrets.

timeless thoughts of a believer

Fajr

Oh Allah, forgive me for oversleeping. Because You listened every time I was weeping. I am ashamed that the blanket has been so heavy. I am ashamed for the times I haven't been ready. I wish I understood the reward of Fajr sooner. Maybe I would have had a better future. Alhamdulillah, now I can't start my day without it, missing Fajr salah left a gap in my heart. I know better now, and I wish I could restart. Because the peace I feel at Fajr, is a peace that I can't explain. And it's certainly a peace I wish to retain.

Jundab b. 'Abdullah reported Allah's Messenger (ﷺ) as saying: He who prayed the morning prayer (in congregation) he is in fact under the protection of Allah. And it can never happen that Allah should demand anything from you in connection with the protection (that He guarantees) and one should not get it. He would then throw him in the fire of Hell. (Sahih Muslim 657a)

timeless thoughts

there is no god worthy of worship,
except Allah. my love for Allah,
is infinite, it knows no limits.

timeless thoughts of a believer

Oh Lord,
please bring comfort,
to my heart and body,
because i have always,
needed you.

timeless thoughts

this dunya is,
just a transit.

timeless thoughts of a believer

Traveller

Remember, you are just a mere traveller in this animation. You don't need to seek this dunya's validation. Do the good that is within your capabilities. So, you can have faith without being fixated on the possibilities. Don't embrace this world. Don't chase this world. And don't worry your soul over that which you can't control. Because Allah is sufficient for your soul.

`Abdullah bin `Umar said, "Allah's Messenger (ﷺ) took hold of my shoulder and said, 'Be in this world as if you were a stranger or a traveller." The sub-narrator added: Ibn `Umar used to say, "If you survive till the evening, do not expect to be alive in the morning, and if you survive till the morning, do not expect to be alive in the evening, and take from your health for your sickness, and (take) from your life for your death." (Sahih Al Bukhari 6416)

timeless thoughts

i'm a sinner,
and my sins,
make me feel like,
i'm too far gone,
but Allah's mercy,
is greater than,
i can imagine.

timeless thoughts of a believer

i want to forget my wrongdoings,
i don't want the day of judgement,
to be a day of regret,
i want to repent sincerely,
i want my iman to increase dearly,
because this dunya is chasing me.

timeless thoughts

this dunya isn't worth it,
the dunya isn't a place,
to be proud of,
it is here today,
gone tomorrow,
and desperately,
i am trying let go of it.

timeless thoughts of a believer

i feel at times,
i'm not worthy of mercy,
but Allah loves me,
despite my flaws,
despite my sins,
despite my neglect,
may Allah forgive me.

timeless thoughts

Worldly desires

I'm losing interest in worldly desires. Losing interest in everything because the satisfaction expires. Envisioning sunnier skies and greener grass. But the dreams contained inside are fragile like glass. Glossed with hope but they're never shatter proof. So, I'm deceived with false expectations because there's a lack of truth. I'm losing interest in the emotions I want to experience. Whenever chaos occurs, I'm the recipient. And it's my fault that I suffer from these consequences. I committed sins at my own expense. I've lived the life I shouldn't have; I've been there. I've lived the life of not having a care. Now I'm numb to worldly pleasures. And I focus on rectifying my errors. Praying for my final destination to be heaven. Questioning whether I should be grateful for these lessons. It made my love for my faith greater. And it brought me back to my Creator.

timeless thoughts of a believer

this dunya will never,
give you justice.

timeless thoughts

i've spent endless nights,
begging Allah,
to save me.

timeless thoughts of a believer

Tired

I'm tired of this dunya, tired of these expectations. Tired of chasing the creation. Tired of worrying about reputations. And maintaining sour reservations. Tired of being trapped by society. And dealing with the anxiety. Every other day tempts me into handing in my resignation. Because this dunya tempts me with illicit compensation. I'm tired of falling behind on my deen. And not knowing what anything means. This dunya has hurt me and left wounds that will never heal. And I'm desperately trying to escape the way it makes me feel. This dunya is leading me to hell, so it's a constant battle. The trials that are thrown my way are difficult to tackle. I'm trying my best to detach myself. It's only possible with the Lord's help.

timeless thoughts

this dunya is,
claustrophobic.

timeless thoughts of a believer

may Allah keep us away,
from everything that is unlawful.

timeless thoughts

wherever you are in your deen,
at your lowest or your highest,
even if your sins stack up above mountains,
come back to Allah,
there is no reason not to come back.

timeless thoughts of a believer

may Allah strengthen,
your iman to the point,
it becomes indestructible,
against shaytaan.

timeless thoughts

the highest levels of Tawakkul,
will surprise you,
with miracles.

timeless thoughts of a believer

don't tire your heart with worry,
put your heart's trust in Allah.

timeless thoughts

Tawakkul

Please don't falter in your submission. He knows everything, nothing happens in this world without His permission. Reliance on Allah will bring you closer to Him, Allah loves those who rely on Him. He is the reason for our hearts, our minds, and our limbs. We are simply the creation. Therefore, Tawakkul is an obligation. We can only increase our Tawakkul by increasing our knowledge in Allah. By understanding the omnipotence and omniscience of Allah. It is through Tawakkul that our hearts find peace. Because Allah is the reason for our inception to this world and for when our hearts cease. Trust in Allah will provide you with Allah's love. Because when you trust in Allah, you will realise it is enough. The more you trust in Allah, the more your Iman will elevate. And the closer it will bring you to Jannah's gates. Tawakkul is a gift; a blessing that will reward you in this world and the next. Tawakkul is a reflection of your faith and conviction in Allah for this dunya's test. It is the armour you need for the battles against shaytaan. It is the sword you need for the battles against shaytaan. Trust in Allah means you have nothing to fear, except Allah. Build and build on your Tawakkul because the scope for it, is limitless.

Say, "Nothing will befall us except what Allah has decreed for us; He is our Protector." So in Allah let the believers put their trust. (Quran, 9:51)

Anas bin Malik narrated that a man said: "O Messenger of Allah! Shall I tie it and rely (upon Allah), or leave it loose and rely (upon Allah)?" He said: "Tie it and rely (upon Allah)." (Jami At Tirmidhi 2517)

timeless thoughts of a believer

don't let this dunya,
blacken your heart.

timeless thoughts

attach your heart,
to Allah,
and nothing in this world,
can destroy you.

timeless thoughts of a believer

Faith

My faith never fails me especially during each storm. When the burdens arise, they always transform. I always remember faith when I'm living with fear. I'm guilty of it but my prayers become more sincere. When the temperature is rising, faith keeps me cool. Snapping me back to reality when I start acting like a fool. Faith humbles me when I forget my lessons. Knocking me back down into making a confession. Being honest with myself when I become reckless. Forcing me to be calculated when I feel helpless. Pressurising me to be strong even at my weakest. Healing me even when my wounds feel like the deepest. Faith has been my surgeon when my heart has stopped. Acting as helping hands when my soul has dropped. Accompanying me when I hit rock bottom. Reminding me that I've never been forgotten. My faith has never failed me in a world that's so cold. So, my faith will stay solid even when I grow old.

Allah is the Guardian of the believers—He brings them out of darkness and into light. As for the disbelievers, their guardians are false gods who lead them out of light and into darkness. It is they who will be the residents of the Fire. They will be there forever. (Quran 2:257)

timeless thoughts

in your hardest battles,
don't lose hope,
don't lose faith,
hold on forever,
and Allah will rescue you.

timeless thoughts of a believer

Sabr

Hold on a little longer, you will get through your struggles. You'll find blessings after all of the trouble. Having Sabr will stop you from doing something you regret. Don't let the shaytaan make you forget. It's a constant battle not to let your impatience control you. Don't rely on this dunya, let Allah console you. You may spend endless nights in tears. You may spend endless nights fighting your fears. Calamities may be on top of your shoulders. But you mustn't forget that Allah has granted you the strength to carry these boulders. Sabr is beautiful and it comes with blessings that you can't imagine. With Tawakkul and Sabr, the most beautiful miracles can happen.

Narrated Anas: Prophet Muhammad ﷺ said "The real patience is at the first stroke of a calamity." (Sahih Al Bukhari 1302, Jami At-Tirmidhi 987 and Sunan an-Nasa'i 1869)

timeless thoughts

may your sabr be rewarded,
in the most beautiful of ways.

timeless thoughts of a believer

my hardships have,
brought me to tears,
into prostration to Allah,
hoping and praying,
for the better days of this dunya,
and for the better life in the next.

timeless thoughts

Downfall

I fell in love with this dunya and it became my downfall. It's the reason why my demons continue to brawl. I grew attached to temporary satisfaction. I was constantly tempted by worldly distractions. Until I became tormented with regret. Upset over the shackles around my soul that I'd always forget. I realised money doesn't mean anything if my heart isn't wealthy. And I overindulged to discover my mind wasn't healthy.

Whoever desires the harvest of the Hereafter, We will increase their harvest. And whoever desires the harvest of this world, We will give them some of it, but they will have no share in the Hereafter. (Quran 42:20)

timeless thoughts of a believer

the dunya we live in,
is so fragile and so fickle,
it is a twisted fantasy,
the shell is painted in gold,
the core is rotten in darkness.

timeless thoughts

i had to suffer,
at the hands of this dunya,
i had to break my own heart,
to truly find my way back to Allah.

timeless thoughts of a believer

i've become a slave,
to this dunya,
when i should only,
be a slave to Allah.

Say, ˹O Prophet,˺ "Praise be to Allah, and peace be upon the servants He has chosen." ˹Ask the disbelievers,˺ "Which is better: Allah or whatever ˹gods˺ they associate ˹with Him˺?" (Quran 27:59)

timeless thoughts

as hardships continue to plague me,
my need and want to become closer to Allah,
increases more and more to the point that,
all i can think of is Allah.

timeless thoughts of a believer

my remorse is heavier,
than anything i can carry,
i am ashamed of so much,
i can only hope Allah,
accepts me despite everything.

timeless thoughts

Sorry

I'm sorry Allah, I really am, because I'm slacking. The solid shield around me is cracking. The evil is seeping in, and the coldness is making a return. And the guilt inside is a continuous burn. I have no excuse, but I can't find enough sincerity in my prayers. Soon enough, the devil will become my slayer. It's ironic because I fear going to hell. I really shouldn't fear it, but I'm locked up inside of a cell. I have myself to blame for this state of pandemonium. I question why I place this life on a podium. But this life can end instantly. Faster than a soldier's life in the frontline infantry. I can't forgive myself for being fixated on stress. I forget that You've given these hurdles as a test. Each day I wake up and give up before I even try. Internally I choose to forget to avoid the truth and then I cry. Because I hate the state of my soul and how it has become so cold. There's more to this life and I know that's something I don't need to be told. But I still get caught up in this struggle. Submerging myself inside of a bubble. Losing myself in this world so I can be missing in the next. But I'm dying to reunite with everyone at the end of this test. I'm falling short of expectations but forgive me. Please grant me Your mercy.

Say, 'O Prophet, that Allah says,' "O My servants who have exceeded the limits against their souls! Do not lose hope in Allah's mercy, for Allah certainly forgives all sins. He is indeed the All-Forgiving, Most Merciful. (Quran 39:53)

timeless thoughts of a believer

Allah doesn't forget,
your tears.

timeless thoughts

sujood has brought me,
a sense of tranquillity,
i cannot find anywhere else.

timeless thoughts of a believer

Oh Allah, You have given me,
so many signs,
please forgive me,
for ignoring them.

timeless thoughts

please humble my heart Allah,
before arrogance destroys me.

timeless thoughts of a believer

Allah please forgive me,
for compromising my deen,
so many times.

timeless thoughts

please don't take,
your deen too lightly,
please don't let this dunya,
fill you with regret.

timeless thoughts of a believer

the problem with this Ummah,
is people like me,
my sins and my arrogance,
has brought suffering,
upon this Ummah.

timeless thoughts

i forget that my sins affect myself,
and the Ummah,
how could i forget?
i don't hold myself accountable,
perhaps i deserve the punishments,
of this life and the next.

timeless thoughts of a believer

Accountability

My heart is heavy for this Ummah, their suffering is my suffering. Feeling their pain has been puzzling. The Ummah is like a body, when one part hurts, the rest of it hurts. Witnessing atrocity after atrocity feels like a curse. The pain of the people in Palestine, Iraq and Libya. The pain of the people in Yemen, Somalia and Syria. It never ends and it never stops. And every time my heart always drops. But it's a part of being a Muslim and being human. The condition of the Ummah has resulted in persecution. The problem with the Ummah is because of people like me, because of my lack accountability. Because of my lack of responsibility. Because of my mountain of sins. Because of my patience wearing thin. How can Allah rectify the Ummah's condition if I can't rectify my own affairs? How can anything be rectified if I haven't rectified my prayers? Before I can point the finger at anything and everything else. I must look into the mirror and ask myself. Am I doing enough? Is my heart full of love? Is my mind pure? How can I be sure?

Narrated An-Nu`man bin Bashir: Allah's Messenger (ﷺ) said, "You see the believers as regards their being merciful among themselves and showing love among themselves and being kind, resembling one body, so that, if any part of the body is not well then the whole body shares the sleeplessness (insomnia) and fever with it." (Ṣaḥīḥ al-Bukhārī 6011, Ṣaḥīḥ Muslim 2586)

timeless thoughts

Shattered heart

My heart hurts for the people of Palestine, I can't begin to imagine their feelings. Witnessing the blood and tears, my heart has been weeping. Innocent souls have been displaced from their families and homes. But Allah has taught me that the people of Palestine are not alone. I've felt helpless watching brothers and sisters trapped under rubble. But the least I can do is make dua that Allah eases their struggles. The Ummah is like one body, when one part hurts, all of it hurts. So even if the pain feels like a curse. Allah grants justice to the fallen, so I know I mustn't be sad for the dead. I should be sad for the living because their suffering lives on in their head. My heart extends to every father, every mother, every son, and every daughter. I ask Allah that your faith never falters. And it's not my duas alone, the Ummah stands with them all. As long as the Ummah stands, Palestine will never fall. The martyrs will always be triumphant. Because Allah sees everything and will hold the oppressors accountable on the Day of Judgement. I should rectify my affairs for the sake of Allah. Because my shortcomings have an impact on this Ummah.

timeless thoughts of a believer

my lack of accountability,
has hurt my soul,
it has hurt my deen,
it has allowed,
the worst in me to exist.

timeless thoughts

if i can't hold myself accountable,
how can i expect,
Allah to forgive me?

timeless thoughts of a believer

how can Allah change,
the condition of myself,
unless i change,
the condition of my heart,
the condition of my mind,
the condition of my soul.

timeless thoughts

i've become a firm believer in,
that Allah won't change the condition,
of the people until we change,
the condition of ourselves.

timeless thoughts of a believer

love and peace,
it has become a hole in my faith,
there is no love and peace,
there is no peace in my community,
there is no love in my community,
we just tolerate and accept,
and cover our eyes,
to the disunity and ridicule.

timeless thoughts

i don't have the answer,
to my problems,
but surely my deen,
is the solution,
to all of my problems.

timeless thoughts of a believer

Turn back

Turn to Allah before it's too late. Allah will help you elevate. Pulling you back up from the depths of the ocean. Come back to Allah, He's aware of the concealed emotions. He knows everything including the unknown in your mind. He can see through the mask you hide behind. He's listening to the sorrows you carry inside. No matter how far gone, He's calling you back to His side. Waiting to grant you the wishes you pray for. Testing you so you can ask Him for more. Turn back before it's too late, before you ask to return. You can share all of your concerns. For every sin, Allah forgives as long as you repent. And for the sadness that burdens you, Allah will find ways to make you content.

Say, 'O Prophet, that Allah says,' "O My servants who have exceeded the limits against their souls! Do not lose hope in Allah's mercy, for Allah certainly forgives all sins. He is indeed the All-Forgiving, Most Merciful. (Quran 39:53)

timeless thoughts

turn back to Allah,
before it's too late,
because you don't want,
the day of judgement,
to become the day of regret.

timeless thoughts of a believer

Dunya

This dunya is cheap and worthless. This world isn't supposed to be your purpose. This place will watch you crash and burn. It'll turn you to ashes before you learn. This world was never worth your time, so don't chase it. It's a place filled with sin, if only you could erase it. It will drain you and give you endless trouble. It thrives on your suffering and struggles. I'm tired of chasing a world that doesn't last. A world that's fragile like glass. It isn't a perfect world, it isn't paradise. A life that comes at a price. I'm ready for the next life, because this one has been filled with disappointment. It's a pessimistic outlook but this world wasn't for enjoyment. This world has broken my heart completely. And it continues to harm me deeply. Despite my intentions, I've dropped my expectations. So, I can live in my imagination.

timeless thoughts

this dunya,
doesn't impress me anymore.

timeless thoughts of a believer

we're all human,
we all make mistakes,
but we are unable forgive,
even over the smallest of issues,
yet we expect Allah,
to grant us His mercy,
on the day of judgement.

timeless thoughts

forgiveness is not a weakness,
it is one of the strongest acts,
you can offer.

'Abdullah ibn al-'As reported that the Prophet, may Allah bless him and grant him peace, said, "Show mercy and you will be shown mercy. Forgive and Allah will forgive you. Woe to the vessels that catch words (i.e. the ears). Woe to those who persist and consciously continue in what they are doing." (Al-Adab Al-Mufrad 380)

timeless thoughts of a believer

forgive for the,
sake of Allah,
because a heart,
that loves to forgive,
will elevate you.

timeless thoughts

for the sake of Allah,
please let it go,
let go of your anger,
let go of your grudges,
and you will be shown compassion,
when you need it the most.

timeless thoughts of a believer

i hope Allah forgives me,
for everything that i can't,
forgive myself of.

timeless thoughts

Repentance

Allah will forgive you if you sincerely atone. He would never let you sink alone. Your sins may be heavy, but His mercy is greater. And He knows what's in your heart as the creator. The remorse you feel means your heart is in the right place. Because you know your wrongdoings leave a stain on your face. And we're all sinners in this world but we must escape temptations. Chasing worldly desires won't grant us elevation. Repentance is a beautiful tool. Ignoring that would make you a fool. But you can't pick and choose. Allah's mercy isn't something you can abuse. You must keep your heart clean in these polluted waters. You must block the devil at your broken borders. And you can't seek forgiveness without salah. As it's a must to believe in Allah. Sometimes you feel like you've become the worst. Trapped in a shell where every action is cursed. But you can't forget that Allah is forgiving. So when you're about to drown, He won't stop you from swimming. Because He wants to forgive you, He just needs you to act on your intentions. He wants to feel remorse in your reflections. Allah can forgive a mountain of sins, as long as your heart is pure. But only if your desire to atone is sincere and sure.

And it is He who accepts repentance from His servants and pardons misdeeds, and He knows what you do. (Quran 42:25)

timeless thoughts of a believer

Allah please forgive me,
for all of my excuses,
because i did not know,
any better.

timeless thoughts

Remorse

I'm sorry Allah, I feel like a disgrace. Endless mistakes build up until I feel out of place. An internal character tainted in misery. I still don't know myself; I am the biggest mystery. The surface is only true to an extent. Under the skin are cells of emotions trying to repent. I pray daily and find myself having these breakdowns. My life is a circus and I'm the biggest clown. My home only contains catastrophes and confusion. I was so blind to the reality, but I can't find any solutions. The soul within has become thin and missing. Blown away in the wind, who am I kidding? Frugal, fragile and foolishly foul. Silent with sorrows, but hollow enough to howl. Laughing at the amusement because this soul barely exists. Literally, it struggles to resist. The Angels are witnessing the free passes to the demons. Whispering in my ears without justifiable reasons. It's pitiful but my history is filled with shame. And I know only I am to blame.

It was narrated that Ibn Ma'qil said: "I entered with my father upon 'Abdullah, and I heard him say: 'The messenger of Allah (ﷺ) said: "Regret is repentance." My father said: 'Did you hear the Prophet (ﷺ) say: "Regret is repentance?" He said: 'Yes.'" (Sunan Ibn Majah 4252)

timeless thoughts of a believer

don't shy away from repentance,
because the scope of Allah's mercy,
is infinite.

Your Lord is Ar-Rahman الرَّحِيْمُ *(The Merciful).*
Your Lord is Al-Ghaffar الْغَفَّارُ *(The Constant Forgiver).*
Your Lord is Al-Ghafoor الْغَفُور *(The Great Forgiver).*

timeless thoughts

Broken

This dunya is lost and broken. A world fuelled by fear until it becomes frozen. People panicking like the pawns that they are. The lack of action is uncovering previous scars. Inserting new wounds for ultimate decimation. Destroying the futures of the new generations. Military diseases to destroy humanity. Elitists watching the expected insanity. Financial crashes will be the real death of us. And the supermarket shelves are showing what's left of us. Empty souls with no faith yet hungry for a solution. Eating to stay safe amongst their own confusion. Isolating away from immunity isn't ideal. But the fools show you what's real. Outnumbering the thinkers in a world plagued by lies. Living to put lives on the line, population control means the numbers die. Don't lose your prayers in these hard times. Because the deaths of the many is one of the first crimes. If it isn't disease, it will be the downfall of extreme capitalism. Followed by a plague of dystopian pessimism. I know the end to this story we call life. We all know what will follow the most extreme strife. That's why it's important to keep your faith in Allah's plans. Or you'll end up in the worst hands.

Abu Huraira reported Allah's Messenger (ﷺ) as saying: The world is a prison-house for a believer and Paradise for a non-believer. (Sahih Muslim 2956)

timeless thoughts of a believer

Pain

Allah will take away your pain, it just requires patience. The pain moulds you into your best self so it's just an expense. The troubling times teach you how to thrive. Setting up your soul to survive. The pain is given to teach you how to cope. It trains your stability to cross the thinnest ropes. Some pain ends and some pain act as permanent reminders. Softening your soul so that you become kinder. Because sometimes the pain hardens your heart into an ugly mess. Admitting that it has broken you is hard to confess. It breaks you down until you feel little. Messing with your heart, soul, and mind, with your emotions missing in the middle. Pain can haunt you. That same pain can taunt you. But this pain was given as a test. Teaching you lessons that you'll treasure in your chest. Sometimes this pain makes you feel like you've had enough. But Allah will take away your pain, so don't give up. It will take time, but things will get better. Especially as you won't feel this pain forever.

and provide for them from sources they could never imagine. And whoever puts their trust in Allah, then He ˹alone˺ is sufficient for them. Certainly Allah achieves His Will. Allah has already set a destiny for everything. (Quran 65:3)

timeless thoughts

my sins have darkened,
the inside of my heart,
sometimes it feels like,
i'm not worthy of forgiveness.

Abu Hurairah narrated that: the Messenger of Allah (ﷺ) said: "Verily, when the slave (of Allah) commits a sin, a black spot appears on his heart. When he refrains from it, seeks forgiveness and repents, his heart is polished clean. But if he returns, it increases until it covers his entire heart. And that is the 'Ran' which Allah mentioned: 'Nay, but on their hearts is the Ran which they used to earn.'" (Jami` at-Tirmidhi 3334)

timeless thoughts of a believer

Allah only You can understand,
what's truly in my heart.

Say, 'O Prophet,' "Whether you conceal what is in your hearts or reveal it, it is known to Allah. For He knows whatever is in the heavens and whatever is on the earth. And Allah is Most Capable of everything." (Quran 3:29)

timeless thoughts

i am a sinner,
but i am a believer,
i seek repentance,
for Allah is the Most Merciful.

timeless thoughts of a believer

the heaviness in your heart,
hurts to carry,
but running back to Allah,
will lessen the weight,
that drags you down.

timeless thoughts

i hope Allah sees the pain,
i carry in my heart,
i hope Allah understands,
the reasons for everything,
that i've become.

timeless thoughts of a believer

Trying

I hope Allah forgives me this Ramadan because I'm filled with sins. Sins that stack up like mountains upon my skin. Infected like a plague that I haven't been able to cure. Inside is a darkened heart that's become impure. I know I've learnt my lessons, but the guilt always burns. Now, the devil is in chains, but the whispers take their turns. The broken mind is because of everlasting heavy rainfall. I repeat the sins and that's become so painful. The barriers of the riverbanks have disintegrated. Any resistance I built up has been eliminated. I worry that when Ramadan ends, I'll be facing floods. The demons will march in one by one so they can spill my blood.

timeless thoughts

May our souls reach Ramadan

I hope our souls reach Ramadan this year. Because we're in a time where there is so much fear. Uncertain and unforeseeable futures have added to the panic. No one foresaw these repercussions being volcanic. Do we deserve this for our sins? Is this the first of many before the end begins? Maybe our souls are covered in too many stains. Maybe we've caused each other too much pain. Is it a sign because we never learn? Have we caused humanity to burn? I hope our souls reach Ramadan so that we can survive. I think we urgently need cleansing to feel alive. We need to stay safe in this harsh climate. We need to maintain our faith as this world goes quiet. We're trapped inside this well deserved isolation. But we need to deserve salvation. I hope we can come closer to the Lord. But until then as a whole, humanity has a lot to work towards.

It was narrated that Abu Hurairah said: "The Messenger of Allah (ﷺ) said: 'There has come to you Ramadan, a blessed month, which Allah, the Mighty and Sublime, has enjoined you to fast. In it the gates of heavens are opened and the gates of Hell are closed, and every devil is chained up. In it Allah has a night which is better than a thousand months; whoever is deprived of its goodness is indeed deprived.'" (Sunan an-Nasa'i 2106)

timeless thoughts of a believer

For the best

I pray this Ramadan I change for the best. I pray that my emotions get some rest. Through prayer I hope I find peace. And I hope that my duas are answered to put my heart at ease. I look forward to pouring my heart out in prostration. And staying away from my vices with sincere dedication. Times are strange with Ramadan being contained in the home. But if you feel lonely, I assure you that you're not alone. I hope you become closer to Allah in isolation. And that being at home doesn't cause your faith any limitations. May your souls be filled with generosity and sincerity. And may this time allow your faith to bring you prosperity. May your prayers ease your heart and may your fasts cleanse your soul. This year I hope you're able to make the most of Ramadan by taking full control. Strengthen your faith and heal. And ensure that your intentions are real.

Narrated Abu Huraira: Allah's Messenger (ﷺ) said, "Whoever observes fasts during the month of Ramadan out of sincere faith, and hoping to attain Allah's rewards, then all his past sins will be forgiven." (Sahih al-Bukhari 38)

timeless thoughts

This Ramadan

This Ramadan, I hope my soul heals. I hope that the vibe is something I can feel. My soul needs mending because it never stopped bleeding. I've only ever fed my stomach when my soul needs feeding. I really hope I can find the right direction. Because the light and I have a broken connection. I just want to feel closer to the Lord. Without having the devil at my neck with swords. The past year has been atrocious for my deen. The images in my head have become so obscene. I want to feel comfort in the masjid. I don't want my prayers to feel invalid. As over many months the sincerity in my heart has felt distant. I just want my faith to feel consistent. And I don't want my fasts to feel like a chore. I don't want religion to feel like a bore. I want to serve my purpose in worship. And to feel a sweetness greater than the sweetest syrup. But more than anything, I want tranquillity. Not just for myself, but for the world to have stability. For the innocent souls that are tortured everyday. I wish for bloodshed in the Ummah to go away. Because for too long the devil's work has abused humanity's fragility. This world is lacking sustainability. So, I pray for the innocent souls to meet the Lord in the highest heavens. Because the evil in this world won't put down their weapons. I say this with complete humility. As I can't question Allah's credibility. I really wish to feel closer to Allah this year. As losing my faith is one of my biggest fears.

timeless thoughts of a believer

Sorrow

I'm going to miss Ramadan because the time just flies. And I wonder if I'll reach the next one before my soul dies. It saddens me that this blessed month will depart. And it worries me that the sins will restart. I spent the whole month trying to escape the chains. I don't want to be trapped in another cycle of pain. I wonder if I've managed to wash away all the stains. Have the demons been permanently slain? Or will they come back through the doors I provide? Because during the rest of the year I struggle to hide. I really hope Allah forgives me for so many of my tainted years. As dying without mercy is one of my biggest fears. This month brings me so much ease and tranquillity. The demons cease to exist, and I finally feel some stability. I'm going to miss the hope this month brings. And I hope the rest of the year doesn't leave a terrible sting. This month humbles my ego and I hope that I continue to feel humility. It's so vital because I seek a life filled with simplicity. And like a bird the month will soon fly away. But I hope the love, peace and positivity stays.

timeless thoughts

Hold onto your iman

Hold onto your iman because Ramadan is ending soon. Unfortunately, my faith isn't immune. But I'm happy with the progress I made this year. I renewed my faith and made my intentions clear. I fought my desires for the sake of Allah. And I regained sincerity within my Salah. Alhamdulillah, I found peace within the chaos I faced. And so many of my doubts were erased. I focused on making my deen stronger. And I wish that Ramadan was longer. As I'm worried that old habits will resurface. But I'm certain that for the rest of the year, I'll remember my purpose. I hope I can hold onto my iman until next year. Because the consequences of losing your faith can be severe. I hope my soul is one that I can save. And may Allah continue to guide me towards the peace that I crave.

The Prophet (ﷺ) said, "Whoever possesses the following three qualities will taste the sweetness of faith: 1. The one to whom Allah and His Apostle become dearer than anything else. 2. Who loves a person and he loves him only for Allah's sake. 3. Who hates to revert to disbelief (Atheism) after Allah has brought (saved) him out from it, as he hates to be thrown in fire." (Sahih al-Bukhari 21)

timeless thoughts of a believer

may Allah accept my efforts,
during Ramadan,
and may Allah allow me,
to witness another.

timeless thoughts

Ya Allah,
i've found myself,
with sleepless nights,
and restless days,
forgive me for not placing,
total reliance on you,
during my most difficult times.

timeless thoughts of a believer

Ya Rabb,
forgive me for forgetting,
the importance of dua.

timeless thoughts

Allah does not forget your tears at night,
He doesn't forget your anxiousness,
He doesn't forget your sadness,
everyone else will forget,
but Allah never ever forgets.

Do you not see that Allah knows whatever is in the heavens and whatever is on the earth? If three converse privately, He is their fourth. If five, He is their sixth. Whether fewer or more, He is with them wherever they may be. Then, on the Day of Judgment, He will inform them of what they have done. Surely Allah has 'perfect' knowledge of all things. (Quran 58:7)

timeless thoughts of a believer

Allah's mercy has,
no limits.

timeless thoughts

Necessity

I need Allah more than anything. I can only be grateful to Allah for everything. He doesn't need me, but I need Him to survive. He provides me with sustenance, He never deprives. But Allah doesn't owe me a thing, I am in debt to Him for eternity. I have all my senses and limbs through His mercy. Allah has granted me all of my hardships and all of my blessings. And I've learnt that this world is depressing. It is a transit; Allah is guiding me to Jannah through His mercy. He has cleansed my heart and soul whenever it is dirty. He has listened to me pour out my pain and stitched me back together. Allah's greatness is infallible, it will last forever. Allah has never failed me despite myself falling behind. He created me from nothing, His authority has never declined. My existence has no meaning without worshipping the Creator. For He is the Withholder, and He is the Elevator. He shows me the path that is right. And when I fall into darkness,

He is the Light. Allah is An-Nur النُّور *(The Light, The Illuminator).*

timeless thoughts of a believer

i'm sorry Allah,
i've missed so many,
of your calls.

timeless thoughts

please don't tire your heart with worry,
instead place your heart's trust in Allah.

timeless thoughts of a believer

Allah knows what you're going through,
He's listening to you, and He's always been with you.

O believers! Seek comfort in patience and prayer. Allah is truly with those who are patient. (Quran 2:153)

timeless thoughts

no one can understand your problems,
the way Allah understands.

timeless thoughts of a believer

Guidance

Speak to me Allah because I don't know what path to follow. I can't laugh when this concrete jungle has me feeling hollow. I just want a route towards the light. Because I've come to hate living in the night. And I don't want to lose my roots on this journey. Or be enslaved to the suits that grant no mercy. I want to fight for social equality. Whilst my family are finally comfortable with financial autonomy.

Never will the Jews or Christians be pleased with you, until you follow their faith. Say, "Allah's guidance is the only ˈtrueˈ guidance." And if you were to follow their desires after ˈallˈ the knowledge that has come to you, there would be none to protect or help you against Allah. (Quran 2:120)

timeless thoughts

don't hesitate,
to ask Allah,
for the impossible.

timeless thoughts of a believer

may your prayers,
be answered,
in the best ways possible.

timeless thoughts

Answer

May Allah answer all of your prayers. May He purify the blood beneath all of your layers. I hope prayers can ease the pressure. And hopefully the peace you find will grant you pleasure. I know happiness is hard to find. But I know it'll be easier when you feed your mind. Mending your soul from this year's damage. I know life has been difficult to manage. But Allah will show you the right passage. So, you can discard any excess baggage. Whilst the demons are locked away. Find a way to sincerely pray. Genuine repentance is important to find some salvation. And stay consistent to gain some elevation. I know deep down you're wishing for an easier life. But ease won't exist without first going through the strife. Be grateful to Allah for blessing you with lessons. Because it is through those hardships that will grant you ascension.

Your Lord has proclaimed, "Call upon Me, I will respond to you. Surely those who are too proud to worship Me will enter Hell, fully humbled." (Quran 40:60)

timeless thoughts of a believer

may Allah protect,
your heart,
from everything,
that isn't good.

timeless thoughts

i've never stopped,
seeking refuge in Allah,
and i will never,
seek refuge elsewhere.

timeless thoughts of a believer

this dunya has,
disappointed me,
more times,
than i can count.

timeless thoughts

in the darkest places,
Allah still finds me,
and pulls me,
back out.

timeless thoughts of a believer

Keep me in your duas

Keep me in your duas, because I don't know where I belong. I don't know how to stay strong. I try not to ask for much, but what I've done isn't enough. I always strive for more because life has been tough. I want to defeat my fears. Bringing an end to dry eyed tears. I keep it together on the surface. But I'm lost without a purpose. Falling apart like autumn leaves whenever I decide to hide. Silence is the only expression when there's chaos inside. I've been at war with the night. And the winter feeling never leaves, so I struggle to fight. My heart is weak, and the anxiety takes over. And sometimes it feels like the end is coming closer. I always ignore the wars. Trying my best to escape through different doors. I don't know my face anymore. Because sometimes I feel like I'm rotten to the core. I constantly find myself swimming to the shore. But I drown in exhaustion as life feels like a chore.

timeless thoughts

Keep me in your duas please

And I've found myself painted in sins. Only I see how tainted I am with these stains upon my skin. These faults are something I never fail to recall. Pinpointing in my life every time I'd fall. Piercing arrows in my chest. Reminding myself that I am far from my best. And that I still have a long way to travel. But I fear it as I don't know what the future will unravel. Keep me in your duas, because I'm on an unsteady path. A difficult path which makes it hard to laugh. So I forget to smile and enjoy. Any pleasure I find, the demons somehow destroy. I need forgiveness but I know it's not something I deserve. As my desires were the only thing I'd serve. Maybe before I die, I'll find the right resting place. And maybe I'll rest without a mask over my face.

timeless thoughts of a believer

may the last sentence,
i utter in this dunya,
be the shahada.

timeless thoughts

Oh Allah, when you take me,
please take me away with mercy.

timeless thoughts of a believer

Wash me clean

When you find my body; wash me clean. Uncover the unseen scars left behind the scenes. Place me onto the shiny silver tray. The one where they place everyone when someone decides not to stay. Inspect my chest and cut away my heart. Carefully remove my organs and discard the worst parts. I can't donate my heart; I just can't donate the pain. I certainly can't reallocate my mind to drive another insane. Wrap me in the cleanest white cloth you can find. Trap me in a casket and filter my mind. Bury me when my body actually dies. And take this as one of my many goodbyes. But I might be too tainted to be buried six feet deep. I might spoil the soil whilst I eternally sleep. If so, keep my body to be burned away from existence. Because my soul and this world needs some distance. If you don't see me in the next life, ask for my name. And I hope my name on your tongue brings you no shame.

Moses prayed, "My Lord! Forgive me and my brother! And admit us into Your mercy. You are the Most Merciful of the merciful." (Quran 7:151)

timeless thoughts

when i'm gone,
please remember me,
keep me in your duas.

timeless thoughts of a believer

when my emotions go cold,
and my heart loses itself,
when my mind stops,
and my body ceases to function,
i will never fail to forget,
Allah is enough.

timeless thoughts

when i isolate myself,
from the world,
that causes constant harm,
He is with me,
wherever i may find myself.

timeless thoughts of a believer

even when,
there is no path left,
Allah will find,
a way out for you.

timeless thoughts

Hold onto your salah

Hold onto your salah, because without it, we're nothing. Hold onto your salah, even if others are judging. Without it, we are powerless. Without it, we risk falling into an endless abyss. A sinner with prayers is worth more in Allah's eyes. They're worth more than a person without prayers who doesn't lie. Because praying is compulsory yet, it's always something we miss. We choose to forget, it's something we choose to dismiss. Just because your sins are so heavy, it doesn't mean you shouldn't pray. Because praying means that you have a chance to wash the sins away. Your life should revolve around your prayers but instead we chase this life. We neglect our purpose in worship and only come back when we face strife. But our salah is timeless, it's our biggest blessing. It calms the mind and soul when we're stressing. Salah isn't only for when we face adversity. But it's our chance to show appreciation and to ask for a chance to be looked at mercifully. Salah is just ourselves and Allah, and it's not a task. It's a chance to face Allah without a mask. Praying is the first step to the forgiveness you seek. And praying will bring you the strength you need when you feel weak. Praying in times of calamity will grant you ease. And praying when your mind is at war will bring you peace. I can't stress the importance of holding onto your salah. Other than that, you hold onto it for yourself and Allah.

Ibn Umar narrated that: Allah's Messenger (ﷺ) said: "The beginning of the time for Salat is pleasing to Allah, and the end of its time is pardoned by Allah." (Jami` at-Tirmidhi 172)

timeless thoughts of a believer

every sinner has a past,
and every sinner has a future,
don't let your sins deter you,
from coming back to Allah.

timeless thoughts

Peace of mind

I pray Salah to find peace of mind. But it struggles to ease my mind. Especially when there's no peace to find. It's difficult when I can't leave the misery behind. Staring into the prayer mat, hoping for salvation. Waiting for Allah to remove these systematic limitations. I pray Salah hoping that it brings these oceans to a standstill. But the glass continues to fall and the emotions spill. The waves break down the walls despite the defensive depth. I pray and I pray but I can't hold onto any strength. I make my prayers and multiply the effort. So eventually I'll find water in the driest deserts. I'm asking for the impossible, but Allah performs miracles. Allah always listens and His love is unconditional.

'Aishah (May Allah be pleased with her) reported: The Prophet (ﷺ) said, "The two Rak'ah before the dawn (Fajr) prayer are better than this world and all it contains." (Riyad as-Salihin 1102)

timeless thoughts of a believer

let your prayers,
wipe away your sins,
let the remembrance of Allah,
wipe away your sins.

Ibn Umar reported: The Messenger of Allah, peace and blessings be upon him, said, "Verily, when a servant stands to pray, his sins are placed on top of his head and shoulders. Every time he bows or prostrates, they fall away from him." (Saihih Ibn Hibban 1769)

timeless thoughts

don't rush your prayers,
for other engagements.

timeless thoughts of a believer

Strength

My Salah keeps me strong. It keeps me sane when things go wrong. Missing a prayer can cause so much damage. It can throw you off-course and make life difficult to manage. Salah is a gift and I wish it was never neglected. Without it I feel so disconnected. It took me years to realise the value of Salah. And why it's important to maintain a strong connection with Allah. I've contemplated hardships and suffered due to a weak connection. And without it, I've been vulnerable to the harshest infections. If I don't purify myself within, how can I expect change? How can I expect peace to be gained? How can I expect the oppression to stop? If I don't fix my faith, the bombs will continue to drop. I need to do better for Allah's sake because my sins hurt everyone else. Sadly, without rectifying my own faults, my duas won't help.

Successful indeed are the believers: those who humble themselves in prayer; (Quran, 23:1-2)

timeless thoughts

may your prayers,
and your good deeds,
wash away your sins,
and build you a palace,
in Jannah.

timeless thoughts of a believer

i feel like a lot of my problems,
exist as a result of my lack of deen,
over the years that i neglected it.

timeless thoughts

it took some time,
but i learnt the hard way,
before falling in love,
with the deen.

timeless thoughts of a believer

please don't let go,
of your deen,
it's one of the last few,
good things in this dunya.

timeless thoughts

i wish i could live in,
simpler times,
because this current dunya,
is not fit for me.

timeless thoughts of a believer

this dunya has humbled me,
it has taught me,
there is little enjoyment,
that isn't deceitful.

timeless thoughts

Illusion

I place my faith in Allah, because this world is an illusion. Chasing this world has only left me in a state of confusion. I've faced failure so often that I've learnt to trust the Most High. I believe in Allah to provide until the day I die. I've faced so many hurdles and affliction. It got to a point where this world became an addiction. I broke the chains by finding my faith. Placing my belief in Allah is keeping me safe. I've fallen several times and that taught me to stay close. And in adversity, success grows. Sometimes it feels like I've been dealt the wrong cards. But Allah never makes things too hard. He provides a way to find success. He shows you the right path for progress. And through worshipping Allah I learnt to appreciate. Being grateful for His blessings meant the struggles would alleviate. You don't have to fall apart by staring at your scars. As your love for Allah will take you far.

The Messenger ˹firmly˺ believes in what has been revealed to him from his Lord, and so do the believers. They ˹all˺ believe in Allah, His angels, His Books, and His messengers. ˹They proclaim,˺ "We make no distinction between any of His messengers." And they say, "We hear and obey. ˹We seek˺ Your forgiveness, our Lord! And to You ˹alone˺ is the final return." (Quran 2:285)

timeless thoughts of a believer

please don't let,
your desires destroy,
your Akhirah.

timeless thoughts

the pleasure of this world,
is a delusion.

timeless thoughts of a believer

anything that is haram,
can never be bring good,
please give it up,
before it is too late.

timeless thoughts

haram only ever,
leads to misery.

timeless thoughts of a believer

please don't be blinded,
by the haram of this dunya,
it only leads to a pitiful fate.

timeless thoughts

may Allah keep your heart,
happy, safe and pure,
may Allah protect it,
against the poisons,
of this dunya.

timeless thoughts of a believer

Ya Allah, please protect us,
protect us from that which you dislike,
protect us from that which you have forbidden,
protect us from Jahannam.

timeless thoughts

whatever you give up,
for the sake of Allah,
He will replace it,
with something better,
something better,
than you could ever imagine.

timeless thoughts of a believer

may Allah protect you from hellfire,
and grant you Paradise.

timeless thoughts

Peace

May Allah grant us peace. May He let the pain cease. So that we can wake up clean. So, we can find a moment where our visions aren't obscene. I hope He takes away your struggles. Uplifts your spirit and takes you out of your bubble. So that your anxiety doesn't result in anguish. I have faith that your happiness won't vanish. Happiness doesn't die, neither does faith. But your cries can stop and the Lord will keep you safe. And I hope those bitter memories don't taint your legacy. I want you to be able to stare into the mirror without seeing the enemy. I want your anger to disappear. And with that, maybe you won't live in fear. Because I know you're frightened of your own actions. I know you want to serve yourself sanctions. You want certainty but the lack of it makes you want to close the curtains. You wish the future was something you could pre-determine. But Allah decides as He knows what's best for your heart. And He loves you, that's why you get the chance to restart. The future starts with leaving the past. But none of this life is easy so I can't tell you how long you'll last.

timeless thoughts of a believer

i'm sorry that i lose myself,
in sujood so often
but there's so much peace,
in sujood.

timeless thoughts

we don't belong here,
we are simply travellers,
in transit for,
our final destination.

timeless thoughts of a believer

Better days

I pray for better days. I pray for the misery to go away. I wish for the agony to disappear. But the anguish exists to torment me with fear. Fears that these wounds will remain. Because I remember I'm tainted with these stains. The strongest detergents can't wash out the curse. I can imagine the darkest auras surrounding my hearse. These issues are deeply rooted in my history. I wonder if the cure is a mystery. But I always come back to my prayer mat. I always neglect myself by avoiding a spiritual chat. It feels like it's too late to be saved. The flaws are permanently engraved. At times I feel ashamed for my story. It feels too sickening and twisted without being gory. I recite Allah's words to feel some sort of chill. Reminding myself that everything is Allah's will. I hold myself accountable for the outcomes. Especially when the guilt makes me feel numb. I pray to relieve myself of a cruel fate. And to live a life that I no longer hate.

timeless thoughts

the reason i pray my salah,
is to worship Allah,
every other reason is secondary.

timeless thoughts of a believer

even if there is an ounce,
of hardness in my heart,
Allah, please remove it,
with haste.

timeless thoughts

Emptiness

Allah, there's an emptiness inside. An emptiness where my demons reside. I tried getting closer to You, but I seem to be getting further away. For once, I wish peace would stay. Allah, I don't know if my emotions are reasonable. But I know they're not seasonal. It's permanent, creeping up when least expected. I'm sorry that my faith feels neglected. But I promise I'm tired of the world that I chase. Often silence fills every space. These thoughts and feelings feel absurd. There's a numbness to every word. I turn to You everyday, because there's no better solution. But my fitness is poor, I need to make a substitution. I don't know what to exchange or replace. Because it's hard enough to show my face. The darkness is taking away everything that was once pure. So, this emptiness is only something Allah can cure.

Narrated Abu Sa`id Al-Khudri and Abu Huraira: The Prophet (ﷺ) said, "No fatigue, nor disease, nor sorrow, nor sadness, nor hurt, nor distress befalls a Muslim, even if it were the prick he receives from a thorn, but that Allah expiates some of his sins for that." (Sahih al-Bukhari 5641, 5642)

timeless thoughts of a believer

Regret

Dear Allah, forgive me for not breaking the cycle. I pray for forgiveness because my sins are never final. Why is it so difficult to avoid the same mistakes? I never seem to learn until the final string breaks. Perfectly imperfect so I could never perfect my soul. I need Ramadan again, to inject light into the holes. I still fall victim to the underlying issues in my pages. This system has destroyed me, and I've tried to rebuild for ages. How do I cleanse my heart of the darkness? How do I make my character harmless? Because over the past few months I've faced too much pollution. I developed bad habits with no possible solutions. I hope I can be worthy of being saved. Especially as I constantly regret how I've behaved. I carry the remorse with a heavy heart. Counting each time, I wish I could restart. Because being emotionless has caused damage beyond repair. So, I'm tired of life feeling unfair. I'm not proud of the person I am, but I know who I would like to be. I just want You to help me become a person I'd like my future children to see. I hope I can be worthy of Your mercy. Because I'm trying my best even when the cycle hurts me.

timeless thoughts

I find myself as though I'm not worthy of forgiveness. And shaytaan wants me to believe I've been inflicted with a sickness. As if my sins are too heavy to handle. As if my sins have turned me into a scandal. I forget that I've been misled into believing I'm lesser than. But the sins that plague me, are everything I'm better than. I forget that I mustn't stop persisting in repentance. To overcome this I had to focus on my own flaws and understand acceptance. I had to hold myself accountable and rectify my own affairs. It took time but I realised that my soul wasn't beyond repair. The work I carried out on my heart was surgical. I accept that I am a sinner and Allah is the most merciful.

Your Lord is Ar-Rahman الرَّحِيمْ *(The Merciful).*
Your Lord is Al-Ghaffar الْغَفَّارْ *(The Constant Forgiver).*
Your Lord is Al-Ghafoor الْغَفُور *(The Great Forgiver).*

timeless thoughts of a believer

Heal

In time, Allah will heal your heart. It takes time to recover after the world tears you apart. I can see how frustrating life has become. I can see how the trauma of this world has made you numb. I know things aren't easy, each day feels catastrophic. Like an earthquake in Nepal that has been so chaotic. Life is hard to balance along with all of the pressures. And it all comes crashing down on you with no room to erase any errors. But Allah will ease those burdens, and I hate to say this, it requires patience. I know you're feeling impatient when your actions are under constant surveillance. But patience is a virtue which will be rewarded as long as you actively work hard. Success will only be found if you move forward. Those sleepless nights will turn into productive days. Each weakness will become a strength that's set to stay. You'll find a way; Allah will guide you towards that goal. Allah will give you the medicine you need to strengthen your soul.

We send down the Quran as a healing and mercy for the believers, but it only increases the wrongdoers in loss. (Quran 17:82)

timeless thoughts

Your Lord is the healer of all things that hurt. He is the orchestrator of the miracles of this universe. With every ounce of pain. We should find ourselves with Allah again. He has provided us with blessings upon blessings since our first breath. And Allah has given us the cure to everything except death.

O humanity! Indeed, there has come to you a warning from your Lord, a cure for what is in the hearts, a guide, and a mercy for the believers. (Quran 10:57)

timeless thoughts of a believer

I've had the darkest of days where the tunnels of darkness never end. Waiting for my despair to suspend, waiting for hope to descend. Wondering when I'll reach a route that will let me escape. And I hold on, searching for faith for Allah's sake. And in the small glimpses where I'm about to give up on myself. Allah grants me His help. He shows me the light and blesses me with a sanctuary. And solutions that feel extraordinary.

Allah is Al-Fattah الفَتَّاح *(The Supreme Solver).*
Allah is An-Nur النُّور *(The Light, The Illuminator).*

timeless thoughts

may you find,
the hope you seek,
in Allah.

timeless thoughts of a believer

Hope

I'll be fine, I have faith in Allah's plans working. It'll take some time, but I'm used to hurting. But facing uncertainty is unsettling. As time passes the deterioration starts developing. I've faced these hardships before. And with Allah's help, I've won these wars. It's depressing now, but brighter days lie ahead. Dark days are temporary, the darkness is just in my head. The worst outcomes make me numb. And I'm weary of what I could become. Last time it was painful, but I managed to survive. Believing in Allah's plans makes me grateful to be alive. I'll be fine, just pray for me. Eventually, I'll be fine, just pray for me.

So, surely with hardship comes ease. Surely with ˹that˺ hardship comes ˹more˺ ease. So once you have fulfilled ˹your duty˺, strive ˹in devotion˺, turning to your Lord ˹alone˺ with hope. (Quran 94:5-8)

timeless thoughts

Every day, Allah blesses us exponentially. And if it not yet apparent, it will be eventually. Sometimes the trials we face, prepares us for the blessing that is going to be bestowed. So embrace the hardships that are imposed. For Allah knows best, and He knows what is good for us at every part of our stories. And He will reward us with glories.

Our Lord is Al-Kareem الْكَرِيْم *(The Most Generous, The Most Esteemed).*
Our Lord is Dhul-Jalaali Wal-Ikraam ذُو الْجَلَالِ وَالْإِكْرَام *(Lord of Glory and Honour, Lord of Majesty and Generosity).*

timeless thoughts of a believer

my heart,
can only find rest,
can only find ease,
can only find peace,
with Allah.

timeless thoughts

my heart at its heaviest,
only finds comfort with Allah.

timeless thoughts of a believer

a heart that remembers Allah,
is a heart that won't be forgotten.

timeless thoughts

I hope Allah can help me build up a wall. One that let's love in whilst standing tall. Protecting me from the cursed world I've grown to chase. I hope I'll respect myself so I can finally look at my face. Ignoring the calls of the devils that ask for war. Avoiding the levels of hell as they always ask for more. I really hope I recover in this state of fasting. Mending the soul with medicine that's everlasting. I hope I avoid the distractions and I pray I stay in line. Preventing reactions that could lead to my decline. May the Lord take my mind once He's pleased with me. So, my legacy lives on when my heart ceases to be.

We will certainly test you with a touch of fear and famine and loss of property, life, and crops. Give good news to those who patiently endure— who say, when struck by a disaster, "Surely to Allah we belong and to Him we will ˹all˺ return." (Quran 155-156)

timeless thoughts of a believer

Ya Allah, i am grateful,
for every trial and tribulation,
Ya Allah, i am grateful,
for every hardship and blessing,
for You know what is best for me.

timeless thoughts

Grateful

Allah, please keep me away from anything that isn't good for me. Because I've made plenty of poor choices with the paths put before me. Please protect me from the bad decisions I make. If I'm travelling too fast, please turn on the brakes. Thanks for not giving up on me when I've drifted so far away. Thank you for lifting me up when my thoughts were grey. I've been in the darkest tunnels, but the light was never extinguished. And when my faith has deteriorated, your love never diminished. I've lacked gratitude but the guidance never ceased. Instead, the blessings have only ever increased.

No soul can ever die without Allah's Will at the destined time. Those who desire worldly gain, We will let them have it, and those who desire heavenly reward, We will grant it to them. And We will reward those who are grateful. (Quran 3:145)

timeless thoughts of a believer

the heart feels,
so much more peace,
once it's detached,
from the dunya.

timeless thoughts

i am blessed to have Islam,
and to be continuously,
guided by Allah.

timeless thoughts of a believer

true love is,
in the remembrance of Allah.

timeless thoughts

Allah knows what's in your heart. He's known everything about you from the start. When you feel lost out at sea, you will never be stranded. He sees everything, and He hears everything, so you'll never be abandoned.

Allah is Al-Khabeer الْخَبِيرُ *(The All-Aware).*
Allah is As-Samee' السَّمِيعُ *(The All-Hearing).*
Allah is Al-Baseer الْبَصِيرُ *(The All-Seeing).*
Allah is Al-'Aleem اَلْعَلِيْمُ *(The All-Knowing).*

timeless thoughts of a believer

Ya Allah, please don't let me,
rely on anything else,
other than You.

timeless thoughts

our Lord is benevolent,
so don't hesitate in asking for the impossible.

timeless thoughts of a believer

Your Lord is The All Powerful, He is The Creator. There is nothing greater. Allah grants miracles, no matter how impossible it may seem. So please don't be afraid to dream. Don't hesitate to ask your Lord for favours. So in the midst of your prayers and duas, please don't waver.

Your Lord is Al-Muqtadir الْمُقْتَدِرُ *(The Powerful).*
Your Lord is Al-Qadeer الْقَادِرُ *(The Omnipotent One).*
Your Lord is Al-Khaaliq الْخَالِقُ *(The Creator, The Maker).*

timeless thoughts

don't shy away,
from your deen.

timeless thoughts of a believer

stay away from anything,
that disturbs your iman.

timeless thoughts

may your duas,
be accepted,
and may your worries,
be eased.

timeless thoughts of a believer

may Allah grant you ease,
in your times of hardship.

timeless thoughts

there is no love greater,
than Allah's love.

timeless thoughts of a believer

our Lord is a Lord of mercy,
so don't give up on His forgiveness.

timeless thoughts

You will meet obstacles in this dunya, obstacles that will test you with anguish. And you will long for these trials to vanish. You will meet people that will bring you agony. But don't despair because your Lord knows what happens in every galaxy. Your suffering and silence doesn't go unreported. Every scar and every wound is recorded.

For your Lord is Al-Musqit ﺍﻟْﻤُﻘْﺴِﻂ *(The Just One).*
Allah is Al-Hakam ﺍﻟْﺤَﻜَﻢ *(The Impartial Judge).*

timeless thoughts of a believer

in every situation,
good or bad,
trust in Allah.

timeless thoughts

the Quran is perfect,
there is nothing better,
that you could read,
it was perfected for you,
gifted to you by Allah.

timeless thoughts of a believer

Forgive me for not opening and reading the Quran enough. For not uttering the Shahada enough. For forgetting You and letting myself get caught up in this test. The world is a poison that darkens what's inside your chest. Forgive me Allah for once not being in love with the deen. For I once didn't understand what it any of it means. Now my love for the deen is overflowing, with the need to improve at every aspect. Never do I want my deen to be something I neglect. I want to worship you Allah in every act of my existence. I've learnt that I can't succeed without your assistance. I want nothing more and nothing less than Your love and mercy. And on the Day of Judgement, I pray that I am worthy.

أَشْهَدُ أَنْ لَا إِلَهَ إِلَّا اَللهُ وَأَشْهَدُ أَنَّ مُحَمَّدًا رَسُولُ اَللهِ
Ash-hadu an la ilaha illa Allah, Wa ash-hadu anna Muhammadan Rasulu-Allah.

timeless thoughts

if you love Allah,
follow the way of Muhammad ﷺ.

timeless thoughts of a believer

Islam has been perfected by Allah,
every answer or solution you require,
can be found in the deen of Allah.

timeless thoughts

your love for the Ummah,
should be so great,
that you feel the pain,
and the suffering of this Ummah,
it should move your heart,
because we should love this Ummah,
the way Muhammad ﷺ loved this Ummah.

timeless thoughts of a believer

there is no compulsion in religion,
but we chose to be Muslim,
how blessed are we to have Islam.

timeless thoughts

the more you learn,
about your deen,
the more you will,
fall in love with Allah.

timeless thoughts of a believer

don't worry about the opinions of others,
worry about what you are doing for your Lord.

timeless thoughts

our Lord does not forget,
and He will hold everyone accountable.

timeless thoughts of a believer

you can only,
find the comfort,
you truly need,
from the Creator,
not the creation.

timeless thoughts

No matter what happens in this dunya, we all return back to Allah in the end. Don't let the temptations of this dunya overwhelm you. Don't let the trials of this dunya consume you. Tests and trials are a part of this life. We're given the hardships of this dunya so that we can be tested. How will we react? What will we do with these hardships? What will we learn? It's easy to be consumed with negativity, it's easy for your iman to become weakened. But I've come to realise, it's all about your perspective. It's crucial to look at this dunya with a different lens. A different lens allows you to deal with the trials of this dunya without as much stress. When you realise the hardships, the tests, the trials, are all temporary, it is easier to become detached from them. Accepting that we all return to Allah in the end, understanding that everything is in Allah's hands, will give you the greatest reassurance when facing this dunya.

`Allah will say to the righteous,` "O tranquil soul! Return to your Lord, well pleased `with Him` and well pleasing `to Him`. So join My servants, and enter My Paradise." (Quran 89:27-30)

timeless thoughts of a believer

Allah's greatness isn't dependent on us,
but we are completely dependent on Him,
we cannot breathe or see without Allah,
we cannot walk or talk without Allah,
we only need Allah, nothing else.

timeless thoughts

Bliss

I have never felt peace and rest the way I felt it whilst in sujood. the peace and rest I felt whilst performing tawaaf is unmatched. A complete break, away from this dunya, just you and your Lord. Raising my hands in supplication and focusing on Allah, it brought the rest my heart so deeply needed. I've never felt so emotionally connected to my Lord until I performed my laps around the Kaaba and my laps to and from Safa and Marwa. My soul felt healed, it felt renewed, it felt like it found what was missing. My stresses melted away, my anxiety disappeared, and my mind was finally able to breathe. Speaking to my Lord brought me humility and it renewed my faith. I asked for what is impossible to humans. I relied entirely on my Lord as one should. I am forever grateful that Allah allowed my heart to fall in love with Islam all over again.

timeless thoughts of a believer

Pilgrim

I miss the crisp air during fajr in Makkah, the sunrising on my way to and from Masjid A'isha. The tiredness that overcame me as I was about to perform tawaaf. The laps to and from Safa and Marwah. Praying salah in front of the Kaaba and how breath taking it was, witnessing it for the first time. The unity I felt with the rest of the Ummah. Asking my Lord for forgiveness, pouring my heart out in dua. I miss it dearly. I know many say they feel like they have left their hearts in Medinah, but i feel like I have left my heart and soul in Makkah. There is no other place where I have felt at ease the way I did in Makkah. I am eternally grateful to be blessed with visiting this holy land and to be granted to rest and peace I needed. I pray that Allah allows me the opportunity to go back to perform Umrah, and that He allows me to one day perform Hajj.

Narrated Abu Huraira: Allah's Messenger (ﷺ) said, "(The performance of) `Umra is an expiation for the sins committed (between it and the previous one). And the reward of Hajj Mabrur (the one accepted by Allah) is nothing except Paradise." (Sahih al-Bukhari 1773)

timeless thoughts

I feel like my heart has changed. Ever since Allah granted me the chance to perform Umrah, to visit the Kaaba in Makkah, to visit the Prophet's Masjid in Medinah. I've grown to feel at peace and detach from this dunya. The pain and void I felt in my heart have decreased, I barely notice it because I've prioritised Allah and placed complete and total faith in Allah. I can't thank my Lord enough for bringing rest to my heart. I wish I had gone sooner; I wish I didn't delay, but Allah is the best of planners. I am eternally grateful for the balance Allah has brought to my heart and soul.

timeless thoughts of a believer

Guilt

I hate that it took me a long time to establish Salah as a way of life. I always told myself, the next day, and then the next day and then the next. I would be filled with guilt each day. Guilty because I didn't perform Salah. Guilty because I was disobeying Allah. Guilty because I wasn't doing my duties as a Muslim. Eventually the guilt resulted in pushing me to perform Salah. But it wasn't good enough, it wasn't sincere. But I told myself at least I'm performing Salah. I prayed and prayed, until it moved my heart. Until I found myself seeking more. I established Salah in my life, but I was slowly establishing it in my heart. Now, Alhamdulillah my soul can't live without it. Worshipping Allah has brought my heart peace and it has brought it rest.

timeless thoughts

in the modern era that we live in,
don't be apologetic about your deen,
stand steadfast in your deen.

timeless thoughts of a believer

Allah didn't create us,
to punish us,
He created us,
to worship Him.

timeless thoughts

there is no hardship,
in religion,
and Allah has perfected,
our religion,
He has granted us ease.

timeless thoughts of a believer

through every hardship,
may Allah keep you smiling.

timeless thoughts

we live in times,
where misery is rampant,
it is often easy to forget,
that smiling is a sunnah,
that we shouldn't pass up.

timeless thoughts of a believer

This life was never supposed to be easy, and I accept that. Despite finding myself closer to Allah, more invested in my deen, it didn't change the difficulties that life brings. It didn't change the tests and the trials that have fallen into my lap. But rather, it changed my perspective. It changed how I feel about the struggles of this life. It made it easier to deal with the hardships. I learnt that this dunya isn't important, but the next life is. I put my faith into my Lord and He gave me the tools to navigate my way through this dunya. So now when I am tasked with hardships, it doesn't faze me like before because my heart is filled with Allah.

Allah does not require of any soul more than what it can afford. All good will be for its own benefit, and all evil will be to its own loss. ˹The believers pray,˺ "Our Lord! Do not punish us if we forget or make a mistake. Our Lord! Do not place a burden on us like the one you placed on those before us. Our Lord! Do not burden us with what we cannot bear. Pardon us, forgive us, and have mercy on us. You are our ˹only˺ Guardian. So grant us victory over the disbelieving people." (Quran 2:286)

timeless thoughts

Allah loves you; He has known of your existence from the dawn of time. You are so beloved to Allah, but this slips your mind. How can you forget that the Creator loves us? Your Lord granted you your first breath. He granted permission to your limbs to function. He granted you life. Allah has always loved you. He has been there with you during every hardship and during every blessing. When hardship falls upon you, Allah is waiting for you to run back to Him. And when you are bestowed with blessings, Allah is waiting for you to thank Him. At your lowest and at your highest, He loves you. Allah loves you more than you can comprehend. Please never doubt your Lord.

Spend in the cause of Allah and do not let your own hands throw you into destruction 'by withholding'. And do good, for Allah certainly loves the good-doers. (Quran 2:195)

timeless thoughts of a believer

nothing can break you,
if you hold complete reliance,
on Allah.

timeless thoughts

may Allah grant us,
unity in our hearts,
and mercy on our souls.

timeless thoughts of a believer

the heart of a believer,
is tested and tested,
and tested again and again,
so that they remember Allah,
so, they can become closer,
and closer to their Lord.

timeless thoughts

how beautiful would it be,
for you and your loves ones,
to be the people of Jannah.

timeless thoughts of a believer

may Paradise be written,
for all of the believers.

timeless thoughts

Clean heart

May Allah keep your heart clean with kindness and sincerity. Don't let the impurities take over and disturb your serenity. Hardships hurt but don't let it make you bitter. Your hardships are temporary obstacles in the river. A few bumps along the way shouldn't stop you from smiling in the mirror. And these tests are just getting you ready for something bigger. So, a clean heart will attract blessings. And don't panic if you find yourself in different settings. Keep your heart calm and strong. And you'll survive when things go wrong. An immaculate heart will help you fight off the demons. Protecting you from the harshest seasons.

timeless thoughts of a believer

Ya Allah,
i'm working my hardest,
to resist my desires,
please don't let me,
fall back into poor habits.

timeless thoughts

Allah gives us,
endless opportunities,
to seek forgiveness,
for our sins.

timeless thoughts of a believer

may Allah,
protect you from this dunya.

timeless thoughts

may Jannah be,
your final destination.

timeless thoughts of a believer

Afterword

As-salamu ʿalaykum wa-rahmatullahi wa-barakatuh.

Thank you for reading Timeless Thoughts of a Believer. The quotes and poems within this book are from my perspective as a Muslim. A personal journey of renewing and strengthening my faith – where I learnt to love Allah and my religion. I hope these words helped bring you closer to Allah and your religion.

May Allah bless you and keep your faith steadfast for eternity.

Rayaan

Printed in Great Britain
by Amazon

21b71589-aacb-4c83-8f20-5fee58dc1dd7R01